W9-BYH-708

Ancient Rome

Ancient Rome

and The Roman Empire

Michael Kerrigan

Dorling Kindersley

London, New York, Sydney, Delhi,
Paris, Munich, and Johannesburg

Publisher: Sean Moore
Editorial Director: Chuck Wills
Project Editor: Barbara Minton
Art Director: Dirk Kaufman
Production Director: David Proffit

Ancient Rome and the Roman
Empire
0-7894-8153-7

First US edition 2001
Published in the US by
DK Publishing, Inc.
95 Madison Avenue
New York, New York 10016

First published 2001 by
BBC Worldwide Ltd.
Woodlands, 80 Wood Lane,
London W12 0TT

Produced for BBC Worldwide by
Toucan Books, Ltd. London

Cover photograph: Robert
Harding Picture Library

Printed and bound in France by
Imprinerie Pollina s.a.
N 80762-C

Color separations by
Imprinerie Pollina s.a.

PICTURE CREDITS:

Page 2 Trip. 6 Trip. 9 Scala.
10 Michael Holford/British
Museum, L; AKG/Museo
Nazionale de Villa Giulia, R.
11 Scala/Musei Capitolini.
12-13 The Art Archive/Dagli
Orti/Museo Archaeologico
Nazionale, Naples. 13 Olive
Pearson. 15 C.M. Dixon, T; AKG/
Erich Lessing, B. 16-17 Sonia
Halliday. 18 Chris Forsey.
19 Trip/B. Turner. 20-1 Michael
Holford. 22 Trip. 23 Michael
Holford. 24 Olive Pearson.
25 The Art Archive/Dagli Orti. 26
Sonia Halliday, T; The Hutchison
Library, B. 28 Scala/Museo
Nazionale Romano.
31 Bridgeman Art Library/Museo
e Gallerie Nazionali di
Capodimonte, Naples.
32 Bridgeman Art Library/Musée
Crozatier, Le Puy-en-Velay.
33 BPK/J. Remmer, T; Bridgeman
Art Library/Louvre, B. 34 Scala/
Gallerie degli Uffizi. 35 Chris
Forsey. 36 Robert Harding/G.R.
Richardson. 37 Michael Holford.
38 Bridgeman Art Library/
Metropolitan Museum of Art,
New York, L; AKG/Erich Lessing,
R. 39 Trip/H. Fairman. 40
Bridgeman Art Library/
Kunsthistorisches Museum,
Vienna, L; The Art Archive/Dagli
Orti, R. 41 Michael Holford.
42 Chris Forsey. 43 The Art
Archive/Dagli Orti. 44 English
Heritage. 44-5, 46 Robert
Harding/R. Rainford. 49 C. M.
Dixon. 50-1 English Heritage/
Paul Highnam. 51 Michael
Holford, L; English Heritage/
Jeremy Richards, R. 52 English
Heritage/Jonathan Bailey.
53 Sonia Halliday/Valerie
Williams. 54 Trip/T. Bognar.
55 The Art Archive/Dagli Orti, L;
Bridgeman Art Library/ Christie's
Images, London, R. 56-7 The Art
Archive/Dagli Orti. 58 C.M.
Dixon. 59 Olive Pearson. 60
Bridgeman Art Library/Louvre, T;
Scala/Museo Gregoriano Profano,
Vatican, B. 61 Scala/Museo
Nazionale, Naples. 62 C.M. Dixon.
63 Chris Forsey. 64 Michael
Holford/ British Museum. 65
Bridgeman Art Library/Museo
Archaeologico Nazionale, Naples,
T; AKG/Gilles Mermet, B. 66
Michael Holford/British
Museum, L; Bridgeman Art
Library/Museo Archaeologico
Nazionale, Cagliari, R. 67 C.M.
Dixon, T; C.M. Dixon,
R. 69 Werner Forman Archive/
Museo Gregoriano Profano,
Vatican. 70 Angelo Hornak.
71 AKG/Erich Lessing, T; C.M.
Dixon, B. 72 The Art Archive/
Dagli Orti. 73 Michael Holford/
British Museum, L; Michael
Holford/Louvre, R. 74 Michael
Holford/British Museum.
75 AKG/Erich Lessing. 76 Angelo
Hornak. 79 Olive Pearson.
80 Les Romains de la Décadence by
Thomas Couture/The Art
Archive/Dagli Orti/Musée
D'Orsay, Paris. 81 Bridgeman Art
Library/Museo Archaeologico
Nazionale, Naples. 82
Scala/Museo Gregoriano
Profano, Vatican. 83 Michael
Holford/British Museum, T;
Michael Holford/ Bardo Museum,
Tunisia. 84 Olive Pearson. 85
Sonia Halliday/Valerie Williams.
86 Scala/Vatican. 87 Sonia
Halliday/Jane Taylor, T; Michael
Holford/British Museum, B.
88 The Art Archive. 89 C.M.
Dixon. 90 Bridgeman Art
Library/Louvre. 91 The Art
Archive/Dagli Orti. 92 Scala/
Museo Nazionale, Naples.
93 The Art Archive/Dagli Orti.

BC	800	700	600	500	400	300	200

ROMAN REPUBLIC

Greeks establish trading
posts on southern Italian
coast

Legendary foundation of
Rome by Romulus

Construction of
Cloaca Maxima

Expulsion of Etruscan
kings; Roman
Republic founded

Golden Age of
classical Athens

Rebellion by
Latin allies

Conquests of
Alexander the Great

Work on Via Appia begun

First Punic War against Carthage

Second Punic War; Rome's
long recovery from rout by
Hannibal at Cannae, 216

Contents

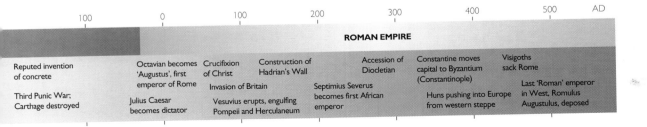

	100	0	100	200	300	400	500	AD

ROMAN EMPIRE

Reputed invention of concrete

Octavian becomes 'Augustus', first emperor of Rome

Crucifixion of Christ

Construction of Hadrian's Wall

Accession of Diocletian

Constantine moves capital to Byzantium (Constantinople)

Visigoths sack Rome

Invasion of Britain

Septimius Severus becomes first African emperor

Last 'Roman' emperor in West, Romulus Augustulus, deposed

Third Punic War; Carthage destroyed

Julius Caesar becomes dictator

Vesuvius erupts, engulfing Pompeii and Herculaneum

Huns pushing into Europe from western steppe

THE RISE
OF ROME

1 THE RISE OF ROME

The civilization of ancient Rome has shaped our own Western world more profoundly than any other. In part, this is because of its longevity: the classical Roman world lasted from the 6th century BC to the 5th century AD, roughly equivalent to the length of time from the early Middle Ages to today. Its legacy is also due to Rome's huge reach: the empire at its height in the 2nd century AD dominated and unified with a single legal system and language an area from Scotland to Egypt, and Morocco to the Caspian Sea, home to more than 100 million people. The Romans' legacy is also seen in their extraordinary building achievements, from military wonders such as Hadrian's Wall and extensive road networks, to the amphitheatres, baths and centrally heated houses that came to define civilized life. Above all, though, the long-lasting influence of the Romans is due to their genius for organization and order.

Previous page: Awesome even in its ruined state, Hadrian's Wall takes the rugged crags of northern Britain in its stride, a fitting monument to the military might and engineering prowess of the Romans.

THE VILLAGE ON THE TIBER

On the slopes of the Palatine Hill in the heart of bustling modern Rome, a sense of ruined majesty is palpable: all around, archaeologists have uncovered the monumental remains of one of the world's great civilizations. From excavations in the valley bottom, though, researchers have recovered traces of a different Rome – an older, much less civilized, less imperial settlement. Here, in what was little more than a cluster of crudely built stone huts, lived a community of Latin shepherds who grazed their flocks in the marshy grounds of the Tiber valley in the 9th to 8th centuries BC, burying their dead in the hut-shaped urns that are almost the only surviving evidence of their existence. These men and women no doubt had neighbourly relations with those who lived in comparable villages on other nearby hills, but there was no sense as yet that they shared any common destiny as 'Romans'.

Large areas of central Italy in this period were dominated by the Etruscans, the native inhabitants of modern Tuscany. It was not until the 7th century BC, under Etruscan influence, that the first steps were taken to drain the Tiber marshes and

1. Rome's Ponte Rotto, or 'broken bridge', was rebuilt as recently as the 1st century AD, but the foundations of its piers date from a good three centuries earlier.

make them the centre of a larger city. With this reclaimed area as its forum or market-place, what had been a series of scattered settlements acquired a single urban focus: the construction of a temple to the Latins' great god Jupiter underlined this. The resulting *urbs* was hardly large, but it now had everything it needed to become the seat of kings – the Latin warlords who ruled the surrounding country on behalf of the Etruscans.

The new state was small and undistinguished, but already it was displaying a certain attitude: in the mid-7th century BC Roman forces destroyed the rival Latin city of Alba Longa. Romans built the first bridge over the Tiber soon afterwards, and founded a seaport colony downriver at Ostia: they were already looking beyond their valley to a wider world. Now they were in contact not only with the civilization of the Etruscans, but with those of the Phoenicians and Greeks, whose ships plied the length and breadth of the Mediterranean. Although the high point of classical Greek civilization still lay in the future, the Greek city-states were well established as commercial centres, and had founded trading colonies in many other lands, including Italy. Along with goods, their traders brought the cultural influences of the whole ancient world – a world with which Rome was now ready to do business.

1. An Amazon (a woman warrior) twists around to shoot off an arrow in this bronze Etruscan statuette.

2. This loving couple are from a tomb relief in the cemetery at Cerveteri.

 ROMULUS AND REMUS

The tale of Romulus and Remus is the foundation legend of Rome. When their mother, a Latin princess, was murdered by a wicked uncle, the baby twins Romulus and Remus were thrown into the Tiber. They were saved by a she-wolf, who suckled and reared the boys as her own, nurturing in them not only a wolf's ferocity but also its pack loyalty. Growing to manhood, they resolved to found a city together, but ended up falling out with one another and ultimately fighting to the death. Romulus, the victor, lived to establish the city that was named after him. The legend even provides a precise chronology: Rome was founded, it clearly states, in 753 BC.

In 510 BC the Romans rose up against their Etruscan overlords, expelled the last king and inaugurated a Roman republic. Although its name was derived from the Latin words *res publica* – literally, 'the public thing' – the Roman revolution was not as radical as it may sound. The common people, or plebeians, were still largely powerless, though governed now not by a single Latin king, but by a group of Roman nobles. These patricians – the city's *patres*, or protective 'fathers' – ruled through an outwardly democratic senate some 300 strong and an official magistrature that invariably upheld the nobility's privileges.

Public life

The highest officials, the censors, drew up the (strictly limited) list of eligible voters, while beneath them the consuls administered the law with the assistance of *aediles*, who took charge of public works, and *quaestors*, who oversaw the day-to-day running of the city's law courts.

Even the humblest of these officials was drawn from the patrician class, and there was never any doubt as to where his loyalties would lie. The resulting class struggle lasted a century and a half, as the discontented plebeians sought to increase their influence. As Rome's importance as an urban centre grew, a new class of successful merchants came to the fore, giving this struggle new impetus. The appointment of 'tribunes of the people' and a popular assembly in 494 BC marked an advance towards more representative government, but it by no means resolved the underlying class struggle.

EXPANSION IN ITALY

Rome's leaders quickly adopted an expansionist policy towards the city's Latin neighbours. As founders in 493 BC of the Latin League, a grouping formed to resist renewed Etruscan domination, the Romans assumed the leadership of the various Latin city-states. Alliance shaded imperceptibly into domination as the 5th century gave way to the 4th century. The threat posed by the Etruscan city of Veii, at that time as large and influential as Rome itself, was neutralized by its capture and destruction in 396 BC. By 351, the Roman-led League had also defeated two other Etruscan cities – Tarquinii and Falerii. The years 340–338 BC saw a rebellion by Latin allies unhappy at Roman domination, but Rome's victory in 338 made the

1

1. Greek soldiers troop across a 4th-century BC funerary picture from the Greek colony at Paestum, southern Italy.

2. Begun in a defensive spirit, Roman expansionism soon became a way of life. By the 3rd century BC the entire Italian peninsula was ruled from Rome.

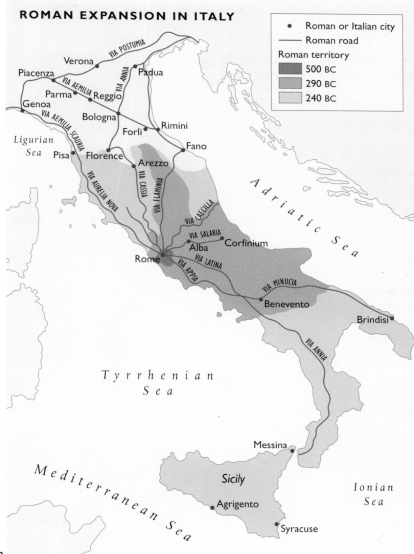

ROMAN EXPANSION IN ITALY

- • Roman or Italian city
- — Roman road
- Roman territory
  - 500 BC
  - 290 BC
  - 240 BC

Verona
VIA POSTUMIA
Piacenza
VIA ANNIA
Padua
VIA AEMILIA
Parma
Reggio
Genoa
Bologna
VIA AEMILIA SCAURIA
Rimini
Forli
Fano
Ligurian Sea
Pisa
Florence
Arezzo
VIA AURELIA NOVA
VIA CASSIA
VIA FLAMINIA
VIA CAECILIA
VIA SALARIA
Alba
Corfinium
Rome
VIA LATINA
VIA APPIA
VIA MINUCIA
Benevento
Brindisi
VIA ANNIA

Adriatic Sea

Tyrrhenian Sea

Messina

Sicily

Agrigento

Syracuse

Mediterranean Sea

Ionian Sea

2

city master of central Italy. In the course of the next 50 years or so, Roman forces not only defeated the Etruscans once and for all, but also suppressed in turn the Samnites, the Umbrians and all the other peoples of mainland Italy.

The Greek colonies in Italy also came under Roman rule, despite the best efforts of Pyrrhus, king of the Greek-speaking kingdom of Epirus in the western Balkan peninsula, who had himself coveted the colonies around Italy's southern coast. Partly by his own brilliant generalship, Pyrrhus humiliated Rome's legions time and again, but at a cost in casualties his forces could not sustain. Roman reinforcements kept arriving, and in the end Pyrrhus was forced to withdraw: his experience has ever since been known as a 'Pyrrhic victory'.

Rome's achievement was remarkable: no other state of the time could have put so many soldiers, fully supplied with equipment and provisions, into the field so quickly. But Roman rule was not exclusively established by military conquest. Many tribes and city-states entered into what they subsequently found were unequal alliances: shrewd diplomacy was just another weapon in the Roman armoury. Yet even the most peaceable of Roman overtures was always backed up by the threat of force – and Rome's army seemed to grow in ferocity with every campaign it fought.

The new army

From the very start, Rome had grown up in the shadow of Etruscan rule, and it had also had to assert its autonomy among a jostling crowd of Latin allies, so a certain militarization of its citizens is easy to understand. A less warlike state would scarcely have endured intact into the 5th century, far less risen to prominence in the Italian peninsula as a whole. But fierce resolve was not enough: Roman military expertise also had to be adaptable.

Rome had inherited from its former Etruscan masters the Greek phalanx, a tight-packed formation of heavily armoured infantrymen with long spears. The phalanx was a fearsome unit, capable of smashing by sheer momentum any opposing formation, but it was cumbersome and vulnerable to attack from the side or behind – something more mobile and flexible was needed. As early as 451 BC, the phalanx was subdivided into smaller 'centuries' to increase its manoeuvrability, but in the 4th century, with Etruria (modern Tuscany) eclipsed, the need for more drastic changes became urgent. Roman armies now found themselves fighting on far less favourable terrain

 Mars, the Romans' god of war, was originally an agricultural deity. The switch marks the militarization of a race that had started out as shepherds and farmers.

1. Tight drill was the key to Roman military success. Here legionaries form the famous 'tortoise' with serried shields – proof against the thickest shower of enemy missiles.

2. Sword drawn and shield thrust forward, a Roman legionary frowns in concentration as he prepares to face the foe.

against the less predictable, faster-moving soldiers of Italy's hill tribes. Thus was born the legion, looser in structure than the phalanx, but bound together by the tightest of drilled-in discipline.

The legion's 4500-odd men comprised three distinct categories of infantrymen, with a set order of battle: a first line of *hastati* or 'javelin men', a second line of *principes*, and a third of experienced *triarii*. The *hastati* were the youngest and least experienced troops. Each was armed with two throwing spears – either the *hasta* (heavy javelin), or the uniquely Roman *pilum*. The latter was almost 3 m (10 ft) long, with a metal shaft that bent on impact so that it could not be returned or easily ˍˍracted from an enemy shield. After throwing ˍˍˍˍavelins, the *hastati* used swords for close-

quarter combat. If the enemy line stood firm, the *hastati* would melt away through their own lines, allowing their similarly equipped but more seasoned elders, the *principes*, to take up the initiative. Should their attack also fail to break the enemy formation, the *principes* in turn slipped back behind a defensive wall formed by the veteran *triarii*. When implemented with the impeccable discipline that was Rome's secret weapon, these straightforward tactics proved devastatingly effective against almost any enemy formation.

A regimented society

Military discipline also had its part to play in peacetime. Wherever Roman power extended in Italy, the duty of military service was demanded in return for the privileges of Roman citizenship, thus investing all Roman citizens with a common *esprit de corps*. The *coloniae* (colonies) that were set up in newly conquered territories were modelled on Rome itself, with their own local senates, consuls and committees of the people, and were pervaded with the same discipline.

The colonies were allowed a considerable degree of autonomy. It is as if the Romans conscripted the very countryside they conquered: just like the army, new territories were subdivided by 'centuriation'. Carved into equal blocks of land, the territories were distributed among Roman settlers – mostly veteran soldiers at the end of their time in the legions. This system encouraged enthusiasm in the ranks, and ensured the long-term presence of a trained and loyal Roman class of yeoman farmers.

THE ROMAN WAY

When censor Appius Claudius started construction of the Via Appia in 312 BC, he was inaugurating what became one of Rome's most distinctive and decisive achievements. Thrusting south and east into the heart of southern Italy, and on down to the coast facing Sicily and North Africa, this great road opened the way to crucial conquests in the decades that followed.

Wherever it campaigned, the Roman army left behind an astonishing system of roads. Major engineering works built for permanence, many of these have provided the foundations for later roads and railways. The central nervous system of the

1

Roman administration, roads were always first and foremost a military asset. Allowing the movement of men and materials with ease and speed, they made possible military deployments wherever they were most needed – if necessary, the switching of forces from one front to another at short notice. Messages could be carried along these routes by mounted couriers at a rate of 160 km (100 miles) a day, while marching troops could cover 48 km (30 miles) or more in a five-hour stint.

Many thousands of kilometres of roads were eventually built: if anything, they represent a greater and more significant achievement than any Roman palace or public building. More than this, though, the Roman road's awesome straightness,

its disdain for local landholding traditions, and its apparent unconcern for the landscape it crossed made it both a symbol and a manifestation of Roman confidence and voracity for conquest.

Building a road

Roman roads took different forms in different places, depending on the materials to hand and the particular problems posed by the terrain. However, it is possible to outline the basic roadbuilding techniques used by the military engineers.

For ease of drainage the typical Roman road was raised above the surrounding landscape on an agger, or foundation of rough-cut rubble. A series

1. As illustrious a monument in its way as his famous Roman column, Trajan's road from Aleppo to Antioch, Syria, was so beautifully constructed as scarcely to register the passage of time.

2. The peaceful Via Appia today belies the warlike origins of this first great Roman road along which men and materials once poured into southern Italy.

ext...
their ja...

2

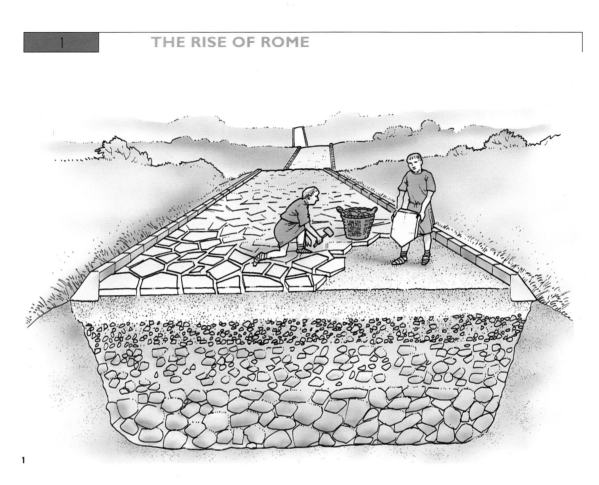

1

of flat slabs on either side made a wall for this base, while ditches dug for roadbuilding ballast doubled as deep gutters to carry off rainwater. On top of the central raised embankment, which was 1 m (3 ft) or more high, a thick layer of sand or gravel was tamped firmly down to provide resilience for the metalled surface above. And 'metalled' it might literally be: in some mining areas, it is reported, discarded iron slag was crushed and spread out smoothly on the roadbed. Over time, exposed to air and rainfall, the iron content rusted together and the entire mass congealed into a hard and very durable travelling surface. Elsewhere, roads might be paved with anything from gravel, crushed flint or limestone, to flat-slab paving stones.

Ruts were often deliberately carved into the road to provide a guiding track for heavy carts and to minimize the risk of slippage in treacherous conditions. Carters had to proceed with special care because roads tended to be steeply cambered for drainage – a road 4 m (13 ft) wide might well drop away 30 cm (12 in) or more to either edge.

A section of ground on each side of the highway was kept clear of buildings, trees, bushes and other obstructions. It seems that this was partly intended to allow for optimum water run-off and partly to provide wayside grazing for draught animals. But it was important, too, for keeping sightlines open, and for lessening the risk of ambush in remote and potentially hostile areas.

Some regions were hostile for reasons other than the attitude of their inhabitants: soft, boggy ground makes roadbuilding extremely difficult; rugged upland is in some ways worse. Low-lying wetlands were crossed, then as now, by raised causeways, but these were no mere embankments of piled-up earth. Roman engineers underpinned their rock-and-earth embankments with timber frameworks, giant cross-beams supporting continuous joists upon which a bed of tree-trunks could then be laid. Mountainous territory posed a different set of problems: deep cuttings had to be dug, and sometimes even tunnels were excavated. But, where possible, such laborious options were avoided: though Roman surveyors sighted out roads in straight sections, these were often gently zigzagged past the more difficult obstructions.

An over-arching achievement

Rivers, streams, ravines and gorges could not so easily be bypassed, but the Romans found few rivers their engineers could not successfully bridge. The use of arch technology made bridgebuilding (and, for that matter, many other forms of construction) comparatively easy. While Greek builders seem to have been the first to develop the arch of interlocking stone, intrigued by its ▷▷

1. Ingenious in its simplicity, the basic construction of the Roman road could be adapted to just about any terrain, from boggy low ground to rocky uplands and arid deserts.

2. Offering strength without solidity and weight, the arch made possible all sorts of astounding engineering achievements, such as this celebrated aqueduct at Segovia, Spain.

Previous page: The deep gorge of the Gardon river in southern France posed no problems for the Roman engineers, who in AD 14 spanned it with this magnificent aqueduct.

1. The arch could be ornamental as well as useful: here it forms the imposing entrance to the great amphitheatre built by the Romans in the 1st century AD at Palmyra, Syria.

1

gravity-defying properties and pleased by its gracefully curved appearance, they made no attempt to explore its load-bearing capabilities.

It was left to the Etruscans to develop the technique of using an enlarged central keystone as a sort of wedge to divert downward pressure sideways, allowing masses of masonry to vault over open spans. They, too, however, reserved what is now known as the 'Roman arch' largely for ornamental uses. When skilfully slotted together, the stones of an arch can stand up of their own accord,

but in general mortar was used, or iron clamps, to be doubly sure. Where a single span was not sufficient to cross a river, two or more arches had to be used, which introduced the tricky task of raising a solid pier in deep running water. In fact, Roman engineers were quite untroubled by this problem: they simply set up a framework of wooden laths and rushes in midstream in the spot required, caulked it with clay so that it was watertight, and then bailed out the enclosure to create a dry working area. Their version of a 3rd-century BC

Greek invention, the 'Archimedes screw', came in very handy here: its spiralling iron blade raised water with great efficiency through a tight cylindrical casing.

A toe in the water

Surprisingly, although the Roman roads were of enormous strategic and administrative benefit, they seem to have done little for the economic life of Roman Italy. Horses were comparatively scarce in the ancient world and were far too precious to be wasted on heavy haulage, for which oxen, donkeys or mules had to be used instead. Large-scale movement of goods was much too slow and expensive for private entrepreneurs.

The roads were effectively reserved for supplying the army, and for servicing a few large public works projects. Moreover, because they were primarily military in their conception, Roman roads were designed to link command centre and frontier, largely disregarding the particular interests of intervening territories. Trade and agricultural production remained, for the most part, local matters. Each colony lived largely on what was yielded by the centuriated lands around it, serviced by its own craftsmen and trading with the wider world only on a small scale through its own merchants.

If Rome was really going to develop its economic power, it was clearly going to have to look beyond the land to the sea – where as yet it had little experience. Until now the Romans had been content to move goods up and downriver to and from their port at Ostia: there, such serious navigators as the Greeks and Phoenicians had taken over. To have any real influence in the Mediterranean as a whole, therefore, the Romans needed to reconceive their state as a maritime power. In the event, this revolution in outlook was thrust upon them by the Carthaginians.

 THE CITY AND THE SEWER

For the Egyptians, the architectural high point was probably the raising of the Great Pyramid; for classical Athens, it was arguably the building of the Parthenon. When it comes to choosing the defining moment of Roman civilization, one might conceivably choose the construction of the *cloaca maxima*, the 'great sewer'. The canalization of existing streams into a single drain in around 570 BC not only helped reclaim the boggy Tiber Valley floor for development, but also created a central sewer to carry off waste. The project thus inaugurated two distinctively Roman traditions: an enthusiasm for ambitious engineering projects and a concern for hygiene that was not matched until modern times.

ACQUIRING AN EMPIRE: THE PUNIC WARS

Roman domination of mainland Italy had implications far beyond Italian shores: by making itself master of the former Greek colonies, Rome had set itself on a collision course with Carthage. A former Phoenician colony that had risen to independent prominence, this North African naval power – the city of Carthage was in what is now Tunisia – had for some time regarded the western Mediterranean as its private trading lake, backing up its commercial claims with a formidable fleet, well equipped for warfare. Carthage's empire did not reach very far inland, but it embraced the islands of Corsica, Sardinia and Sicily, as well as coastal North Africa as far as Egypt, while in the west it included a sizeable chunk of southern Spain. Its trading contacts extended far beyond, into the heart of Celtic Europe, down the Atlantic coast of Africa and north as far as Cornwall. The comparative slightness of the empire is in any case deceptive, for if Carthage did not rule much land, it ruled the waves almost unchallenged. Carthaginian relations with Greek traders from the southern Italian cities had always been somewhat strained, but the emergence of Rome, its expansion well established, prompted a crisis.

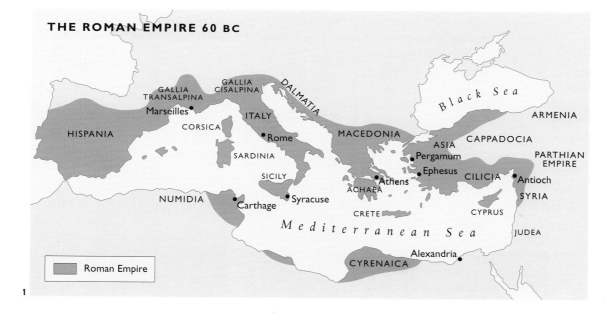

THE ROMAN EMPIRE 60 BC

Roman Empire

1. The acquisition of Carthage's coastal possessions opened up the way to wider conquests for the Romans: by 60 BC they were well on the way to building a sizeable empire.

2. Roman legionaries dwarf their transport in a scene from Trajan's Column (AD 133): 250 years after the smashing of Carthage, the Romans still had difficulty seeing themselves as a maritime power.

2

In 264 BC the Greeks of Sicily became involved in a dispute with their Carthaginian rulers, and the Romans saw an ideal opportunity for making mischief beyond the Italian peninsula.

All at sea

Tension quickly flared up into full-scale war, for which the Romans were ill-prepared, mainly because it was primarily a naval conflict. But if Rome's mobilization for maritime war was uncertain, there is an awe-inspiring resourcefulness about a people who, chancing upon a stranded Carthaginian galley, could simply set to and build 100 copies of it within 60 days.

So much timber was felled for shipbuilding during the Punic Wars that deforestation in the Apennine valleys caused major landslips — and, several centuries later, fatal silting far downriver at the port of Ostia.

Just as impressive in its way was the Romans' readiness to make a military virtue out of necessity: unused to naval warfare, they decided to stage land battles at sea. Each of their new vessels was duly equipped with a device of their own invention, the *corvus* or 'crow' – a hinged gangway that could be swung down to hook on to the deck of an enemy ship, allowing squads of legionaries to swarm across for the sort of hand-to-hand fighting to which they were accustomed. Nevertheless, this device alone could hardly overcome Carthaginian naval prowess at a stroke – especially as the arts of seamanship were proving difficult for the Romans to master. The balance in the First Punic War (as it

 ## A RIVAL TO ROME

The centre of an extensive empire, Carthage had started out as a colony itself, founded on the North African coast perhaps as early as the 9th century BC by Phoenician traders from the ports of Tyre and Sidon in what is now northern Lebanon. They shipped metals from the mines of Spain and Portugal (and even, it is thought, from the Cornish coast), exchanging them in eastern Mediterranean markets for manufactured goods such as pottery and cloth. The Carthaginians appear to have kept up many ancient Phoenician traditions – including, the archaeological record suggests, that of child sacrifice. Other than this, though, remarkably little of Carthage is now known. Most of the surviving evidence comes from Greek and Roman writers, and their degree of bias against a traditional enemy is impossible to judge accurately.

was called from the Latin word *Punicus*, 'Phoenician') tipped back and forth for over 20 years. Finally, in 241 BC, Roman forces dislodged the Carthaginians from their possessions in Sicily. Frequently outmanoeuvred and outfought at sea, the Romans refused to give up: as against Pyrrhus, persistence and sheer manpower had seen Rome through.

Carthage strikes back

While the loss of Sicily was a blow, Carthage had by no means been broken by its defeat. In 218 BC the brilliant young Carthaginian general Hannibal launched an overland attack through southern Spain, thus opening the hostilities in what history calls the Second Punic War. With an army famously including a squadron of 37 elephants, Hannibal marched his forces first across the Pyrenees and then over the Alps into Italy. Celtic tribesmen flocked to his banner as he went, eager to have a hand in Rome's humiliation. Three major Roman counter-attacks in succession were crushed as Hannibal marched on: first at the Trebbia river, then at Lake Trasimeno and finally, and most humiliatingly of all, at Cannae in 216 BC, where Rome lost 45,000 men.

As the conquered territories of southern Italy saw their opportunity to rise against their Roman rulers, the Romans faced complete destruction. Yet again, sheer doggedness saved them – that and Rome's unequalled ability to raise, train and service an army whatever the conditions. By 212 BC there were almost a quarter of a million Roman soldiers in the field. Like Pyrrhus before him, Hannibal had defeated the Romans over and over again, yet it seemed he could not hope to win the war. Far from his Carthaginian home and any hope of reinforcement, he found himself finally defeated, not by Rome's generals, but by its recruiting sergeants and quartermasters. Rome went on to the offensive, landing an expedition on the North African coast, and Hannibal had to hurry back to the aid of his home city.

In 202 BC the Roman general Publius Cornelius Scipio (known later as Scipio Africanus) defeated Hannibal decisively at Zama, a few miles from Carthage. Not only had Rome been saved, but it had suddenly acquired a sizeable empire.

1. The Phoenician city of Carthage, razed to the ground by its embittered conquerors, was rebuilt in the idealized image of Rome: the governor Antonias built these thermal baths in the 2nd century AD.

2. Sacked first by the Romans in a frenzy of revenge, and then ravaged by the elements over many centuries, Carthage stands today as a melancholy monument to ancient wars.

THE EMPIRE TRIUMPHANT

THE EMPIRE TRIUMPHANT

The end of the 3rd century BC might very well have marked the end of Rome, which would have remained one of the more interesting if comparatively short-lived ancient civilizations. Hannibal might easily have destroyed the upstart state before it could make the transition from local to regional power. Scholars would still have studied Rome – rather as they study Etruria today. A combination of sheer good luck and determination had, however, spared Rome from extinction – indeed, it entered the 2nd century BC poised for imperial greatness. With its leading rival, Carthage, now prostrated, Rome undertook a series of quick-fire campaigns: victory over the Macedonians in 197 BC was followed seven years later by the defeat of King Antiochus the Great of Syria. In 146 BC, after rising again to wage the Third Punic War, Carthage was laid waste, leaving the Romans undisputed masters of the Mediterranean.

Previous page: Legionaries battle with barbarian 'Germani' in this elaborate relief. From the 1st century BC Rome's forces pushed steadily outwards from the Mediterranean.

THE RISE OF THE STRONGMAN

After Rome's success against Carthage, the resentment of the Italian *socii* (allies) at the unequal distribution of the empire's new-found power finally resulted in the Social War of 91–88 BC. This war ended in a compromise: Rome won what might have been a deeply damaging conflict, but conceded to all Italians the key status of *cives Romanus*, Roman citizen.

During the wars against Carthage, unrest had been simmering closer to home, where the institutional fabric of the Roman republic was tested to the limits by the perception among many Romans that unprecedented power and wealth were concentrated in the hands of the same patrician few. The spoils of victory against Carthage had served only to heighten the existing tensions in Roman society. When the people's tribune Tiberius Sempronius Gracchus was assassinated, along with many of his supporters, in 133 BC, popular anger boiled over. Suspecting – correctly enough, it seems – that their hero had been murdered by agents of the senatorial class, the people of Rome rose up and were joined by discontented Italians and other provincials.

As the state lurched from crisis to crisis, a number of reformers attempted to take charge – though the first of these, Lucius Cornelius Sulla, was if anything a conservative dedicated to protecting the rights of his fellow patricians. Defeating his leading opponent, Gaius Marius, in 86 BC, Sulla imposed a new constitution in a reign of terror. While his rule succeeded in suppressing popular discontent, he did nothing to end it.

1

1. Roman ruthlessness and thirst for power are personified in this cold-eyed figure of Julius Caesar.

Hail, Caesar

The excessive adulation accorded to the young general Gnaeus Pompeius (Pompey the Great) for his conquests in what is now northern Turkey and Palestine in 64 BC was perhaps a sign of things to come. Impatient with a representative system that had in fact never represented them, ordinary Romans were starting to respond to the glamour of a strong leader. Sensing the shift in mood, the aristocratic Lucius Sergius Catilina (Catiline) attempted to seize power in a coup in 63 BC. He was thwarted, but time was running out for the Roman republic. In 60 BC the First Triumvirate was formed – the *tres viri* (three men) indicated by the title being Pompey, Marcus Licinius Crassus and Gaius Julius Caesar. This effectively replaced the traditional political institutions of the republic. Caesar's conquest of Gaul (modern France), as well as parts of Rhineland Germany, with a brief expedition into Britain in 55 BC, not only extended the empire into

1

In Gaul in 58 BC, Julius Caesar's single legion of about 4500 men took just two weeks to throw up an earth rampart about 5 m (16 ft) high and 29 km (18 miles) long, with garrisoned forts.

rich lands to the west, but also brought Caesar great riches and political power.

Tensions were growing between the fêted conqueror of Gaul and his fellow *triumvirs* back home, however, and matters were made worse by the way an adoring populace allied itself with Caesar's cause. In 49 BC he crossed the Rubicon, the river that marked the frontier of Gaul: symbolically, he was invading his own country. Civil war flared throughout the empire as the different factions fought for power, but by 45 BC Caesar had emerged as sole dictator. He did not enjoy his reign for long: the following year he was assassinated on the Ides of March (15 March) by republican conspirators led by Marcus Junius Brutus and Gaius Cassius Longinus (Cassius).

1. This late 19th-century work by Henri-Paul Motte shows Celtic chieftain Vercingetorix acknowledging the futility of resistance to Caesar's legions in 52 BC.

2. Octavian, crowned with the laurels of victory.

3. The praetorian guard was set up by Octavian to protect him as emperor.

2

3

THE FIRST EMPEROR

Caesar was dead, but his dictatorship lived on as an ideal: the conspirators had fatally compromised their moral case by committing murder, however noble their intentions. Having defeated the republican forces at Philippi in 42 BC, Caesar's henchmen were left with a clear run to power. Unable to agree among themselves how that power should be shared out, they were soon leading Rome in what was becoming a habitual slide into civil conflict. The empire's forces were soon arrayed in two opposing factions, one led by Caesar's former right-hand man, Marcus Antonius (Mark Antony), the other by Caesar's nephew and adopted son Octavian, still a teenager.

Outright war was for a time held off by the division of the empire into two separate spheres: the western part was ruled by Octavian, the eastern by Mark Antony. But the two halves of the Roman world were soon at war. Despite the support of his wife, the Egyptian queen Cleopatra, Antony was defeated at Actium in 31 BC. Octavian then reunited an empire now enlarged and enriched by the addition of the vanquished Cleopatra's kingdom on the Nile, with the vital commercial city of Alexandria on its Mediterranean coast.

A quiet revolution

A natural tactician in peace as in war, Octavian set about transforming Roman government, paying public respect to the institutions of the republic while concentrating their power in his own hands. According himself *potestas tribunicia*, the power of the tribunes, he took on sole responsibility for representing Rome's common people, while at the same time making himself military *imperator*, commander-in-chief or emperor. Such lofty duties required a suitable title, so he took the name Augustus – literally, 'august' or glorious. He also established an élite praetorian guard to take care of his own protection. He was so tactful in the way he went about making these changes that ordinary Romans scarcely seem to have noticed that the much-vaunted freedoms of their republic had been dropped in favour of what actually amounted to an imperial monarchy.

THE ARTISTIC EMPIRE

Yet why should they mind? Augustan Rome might not have been free, but it was strong, prosperous and, above all, peaceful. Many Romans saw the advantage of a government that was at least secure, after decades of civil war. Augustus was resourceful in turning this sentiment to his own account, launching a great public building programme aimed at fostering what a modern politician might call the 'feel-good factor'.

Restoring Rome's ancient temples, Augustus also redeveloped the Forum, laying careful emphasis on the continuity of his imperial Rome with its illustrious republican history. He also

▷ CITIZEN CICERO

The orator whose impassioned speech to the Senate foiled the Catiline Conspiracy, Marcus Tullius Cicero was one of the greatest Romans, but also one of the most typical. In his eloquence and his love of the law he exemplified all that the Roman citizen strove to be. In a culture that saw government as the noblest of arts, rhetorical skill like Cicero's was highly prized; no more worthy occupation could be imagined than to argue for justice in a Roman court. Flexibility of mind was consciously fostered by Roman education: the smart young man was expected to be able to argue either side of any given case with ease. Some things were supposed to be inviolate, though, and the accountability of those in authority was one of these. A hero in 63 BC when he faced down Catiline, Cicero finally ended up a martyr to Octavian's cause: in 43 BC he made a stand against Mark Antony, then bidding for dictatorship, and was executed for his pains.

1

created new amphitheatres, porticoes, palaces and shrines, but took care to give the impression of promoting not himself but his city and its people.

The grand buildings and monuments of Augustan Rome are also striking in their clean austerity, displaying the unfussy lines found in Athens three centuries earlier. Since occupying the former Greek colonies of southern Italy, the Romans had been keen followers of Greek aesthetic

1. The temple of Mars Ultor, 'Mars the Avenger', was built by Augustus in fulfilment of a vow he had made as he hunted down the assassins of his uncle and patron, Julius Caesar.

For all its staggering scale and architectural beauty, its true significance was not aesthetic: attack the emperor, it warned would-be rivals, at your utmost peril.

1

tastes – but these had long since moved on to the flamboyance of post-classical, Hellenistic style. Keen to present himself as a man of moderation and simple piety, Augustus promoted a move back to classical basics.

Mosaics and more

The most distinctively 'Roman' of all visual art-forms, the mosaic, was also in fact inherited from the Greeks. It, too, took off in the artistic explosion fostered by Augustus's cult of civic glory. Mosaic is an essentially simple technique for the creation of hardwearing decorative images by setting *tesserae* (fragments) of multicoloured glass and ceramic in mortar. In the hands of Roman artists the technique reached heights of unimaginable complexity.

2

1

2

1. A Roman noblewoman plays on a stringed *cithera* in this wall-painting dating from around 50 BC.

2. All Roman art arguably pays homage to that of the Greeks, but this bust of Athena does so directly: it is a copy of a work by the Greek sculptor Phidias.

A skilled Roman mosaicist could conjure swirling curves from these angular shards, evoking movement and humanity from their hardness. Great mosaics such as those uncovered at Pompeii not only present a remarkable portrait of everyday Roman life, but they also represent an astonishing testament to the artistic sensibilities of a civilization often regarded as narrowly militaristic.

Sculpture, too, thrived under Augustus: busts and statues of the emperor were an effective way of promoting his cult throughout the wider empire. But his public works programme fostered creativity far beyond propaganda. Wall-painted frescoes flourished again as they had under the Etruscans, but with artistic techniques learned from the Greeks and uniquely Roman experiments in the depiction of space and perspective. Paintings were also created on wooden panels, with subjects ranging from mythology and history to landscape and still life.

Poets of power

Nowhere was the upsurge in creativity that Augustus oversaw more pronounced than in writing. Several of the ancient world's greatest writers were at work in this golden age of Latin literature. An astonishing range of achievement is evident: from the history of Livy to the lyrics of Tibullus; from the stately poems of Propertius to the odes of Horace; from Ovid's eroticism and humour to Virgil's straight-faced Roman majesty.

The ultimate all-Roman poet, Virgil had consciously enlisted in the service of Augustus's empire. 'Remember Roman to rule the nations', his great epic, the *Aeneid* commanded: it was not so much Rome's privilege to rule the world, as its duty. His exiled Trojan hero, *pius* (pious or dutiful) Aeneas, may even have been an idealized icon of Augustus himself as he wished to be seen: unflamboyantly brave, kind and sensitive, but simple and modest in his tastes; the conscientious leader whose life was humbly dedicated to his people.

 A TALE OF TWO CITIES

The eruption of Vesuvius in AD 79 brought disaster to the nearby cities of Pompeii and Herculaneum – until then two prosperous settlements near the coast of the Bay of Naples. Caught completely by surprise, their inhabitants were choked to death by volcanic gases or immolated in the ash that came showering down upon them from the sky. The catastrophe has left us the most striking snapshot of everyday Roman life. Two entire cities were frozen in time by the eruption, with most of their streets, houses and shops preserved intact (as in this scene from Pompeii, right). Eeriest of all are the mummified forms of suffocating men, women, children and animals unearthed at Pompeii. But more significant from an archaeological point of view, perhaps, are some of the finds made at Herculaneum. The lava flows that engulfed this smaller city preserved not only the mosaics and murals of luxuriously appointed merchants' houses, but also all sorts of humbler items, such as wood, leather, papyrus scrolls and even food.

IN THE STEPS OF AUGUSTUS

Although he had taken great care to encourage the notion that he was an unassuming servant of the state, Augustus had little difficulty in ensuring that the position of emperor passed down through his family by what amounted to dynastic succession. In theory, of course, the emperor was an official appointed by the Senate, but the next four emperors all belonged to Augustus's Julio-Claudian family. None ruled without opposition: his chosen heir, Tiberius (reigned AD 14–37), may have been secure enough, but his successor, Caligula, was assassinated by his own bodyguards. Claudius, who followed in AD 41, was probably poisoned, while Nero, who came after him, was murdered in AD 68.

Such turbulence at the top obscures the basic stability of the empire, the northwestern frontier of which, in AD 43, had been extended across the English Channel to include Britain. All these emperors followed Augustus's example, enhancing their own image by public building works: with every reign, Rome grew steadily in splendour. After Nero, emperors were elected and assassinated in rapid succession as one or other division of the Roman army attempted to impose its man: the first really to establish himself was Vespasian in AD 69.

Vespasian ruled for 20 years before giving way to his sons Titus (79–81) and then Domitian (81–96). A weak character who sought to shore up his position by his ruthlessness, Domitian so alarmed his supporters that they finally conspired in his assassination. He and his successor Nerva both died without sons to succeed them, so a sequence of 'adoptive' emperors followed, though in rulers such as Trajan (98–117), Hadrian (117–38) and Antoninus (138–61) the system perhaps found the best possible candidates for a difficult job.

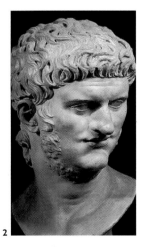

1. Two imperial couples can be seen in this curious cameo: Cladius and his wife Agrippina the Younger (on the left of the cameo) and Germanicus with Agrippina the Elder (on the right).

2. There is a certain desperate air in this bust of Emperor Nero: yet for all his notoriety, he ruled a remarkably stable empire for almost 30 years.

 THE COLOSSEUM

When the Flavian amphitheatre, the Colosseum, was inaugurated in AD 80, several hundred gladiators and thousands of animals were killed in the incredible 100-day festival of bloodlust that marked its opening. 'Bread and Circuses' – the distribution of grain to the Roman poor and the staging of shows to keep them happy – were part of Roman life from an early date. As the empire grew, so did the size and frequency of the spectacles, and there is no doubt that the Colosseum ushered in something of a golden age of gore. The amphitheatre had a labyrinth of cells and tunnels in the basement to accommodate the gladiators and animals and to keep them safely apart. There were trap doors from which wild beasts could spring forth, and ramps and winches for staging spectacular visual effects. The Colosseum brought shows of unprecedented scale and sophistication to audiences of more than 40,000 people.

THE MILITARY MACHINE

As the 2nd century AD progressed, Roman power approached its height, with new conquests in Germany, the Balkans, Asia Minor and the Middle East, as well as Britain, supplementing Augustus's empire. Campaigning across a range of different terrains, from deserts to alpine glaciers, the army had been required to show the utmost adaptability. Although use of the *pilum* and *hasta* had disappeared, the army's core remained the Roman infantryman with a rectangular *scutum* (shield) and a *gladius* (sword). Since the end of the Punic Wars, however, the long-pointed and slightly leaf-shaped *gladius hispaniensis* (Spanish sword) had gradually been replaced by the short-pointed, straight Pompeian sword as the main weapon. The Spanish sword was designed mainly for thrusting at close quarters, but the Pompeian sword was more of a hacking weapon. According to Livy, a legionary attack with such a sword left 'arms torn away, shoulders and all, heads separated from bodies with the necks completely severed, and stomachs ripped open'.

In addition to these weapons, the legionary carried supplies for the road and tools for entrenching: every night on campaign, the army erected elaborate encampments, fully fortified against surprise attack.

Augustus's addition of auxiliaries to the legions greatly increased the army's flexibility and extended its range of fighting options. Comprising companies of heavy or light infantry, archers, slingers or cavalrymen according to local tradition and prevailing terrain, auxiliaries made possible a

swift and effective military response in situations where heavily armed legionary troops were unsuitable or unavailable. As the empire grew in size, the number of non-Italian soldiers even within the legions grew, but the Roman army by now had the structure, and system of discipline, to make legionaries of anyone. The combination of

1

2

flexible auxiliary units with legions drilled to perfection in attack and defence, siege warfare, fortification and road and bridgebuilding, produced a Roman military machine capable of defeating any enemy the empire might face.

The empire digs in

Hadrian's Wall in northern Britain is one of the most impressive monuments to the Roman army. The wall ran for more than 113 km (70 miles) from the Solway Firth to the estuary of the Tyne, defending northern England from hostile tribes in Scotland. The remnants remain imposing: in its day, the stone fortifications, around 5 m (16 ft 4 in) high, must have been intimidating to the local

1. The Roman legionary, shown here operating a catapult, was well kitted out for campaigning. He could as readily do engineering work as fight in battle.

2. Soldiers build fortifications in this scene from Trajan's Column (AD 113).

3. The emperor leads his own forces into action against the Dacians in this climactic scene from the narrative carved around Trajan's Column.

3

1

British people. With additional earth banks on either side, a 3 m (10 ft) *vallum* (ditch), a military road and 80 castles with smaller watchtowers placed between, as well as a number of larger forts, it stood as testimony both to the Romans' engineering capabilities and to the wealth of resources at their command.

Even so, this assertion of military might can also be interpreted as an acknowledgement of the

2

☆ The wheelspan of Roman carts, indicated by ruts they left at the entrance to the fort at Housesteads on Hadrian's Wall, was adopted almost two millennia later by British railway engineers as standard gauge.

limitations of Roman power. Hadrian's Wall may never really have marked the extreme limit of the empire – there would have been several successful expeditions farther to the north, and even another barrier, the Antonine Wall, between the Forth and Clyde. Yet the construction of permanent frontiers such as this, and others in the Germanic and Danube provinces, did constitute a recognition that the long expansion of Rome's territories could not continue. Where now was Virgil's exhortation to Romans to 'rule the nations'? Where was the *pax Romana* (Roman peace) that Augustus had envisaged one day embracing the entire Earth?

For the moment, though, powerful fortifications and an effective strategy of frontier defence meant that the Roman sun shone uninterruptedly all the way from the hills of Scotland in the north to the valleys of Syria in the south.

1. The English word 'chester' comes from the Latin *castra*, or military camp. Here the remains of the fort at Chesters, Northumberland, are seen from the air.

2. The fort at Chesters was one of a series of strongholds placed across the breadth of northern Britain, all linked together by the fixed frontier of Hadrian's Wall.

THE ROMAN WORLD

3 | THE ROMAN WORLD

For more than a century at the high point of the empire, Roman rule remained essentially unchallenged. Palace politics might have been fast and furious, the imperial succession at times violently abrupt, but such ups and downs did little to disturb the smooth running of the empire as a whole. The so-called *pax Romana* (Roman peace) prevailed throughout the Roman world. It was taken for granted that beyond the frontiers lived only uncivilized and barbarous peoples. Within the empire men and women could pride themselves on belonging to the biggest, best-organized political entity the world had seen – or was ever likely to see, for who could envisage such a civilization ending? Even today, more than 15 centuries after its fall, we can still only marvel at the extent of Rome's achievements, and at the awesome efficiency with which a single city exported its way of life across an entire world.

Previous page: Bathing was a vital focus for social life in the Roman world. The English city of Bath took its name from the elaborate bathing complex that the invaders built around the natural hot springs.

ORDERING THE EARTH

At the height of the Roman Empire more than 80,000 km (50,000 miles) of road linked Rome with its most far-flung provinces. Away from the land, you could sail from Ostia to Mauritania, Armenia or even Britain along regular, well-travelled sea routes. While such communications were shrinking the world, so, too, was a comprehensive Romanization of the various native societies that lived within the empire's boundaries. This process began with the physical infrastructure, but also extended through political and judicial institutions to produce Roman attitudes and assumptions and Roman tastes.

Writing at the end of the 1st century AD, the historian Tacitus noted with a certain cynicism how his father-in-law, Agricola, having subdued the rebellious Britons militarily, promptly set out to win their hearts and minds. Throughout the first winter after his conquest the victorious general busied himself with social 'improvement', helping his subjects build villas, temples – whole towns even – in the Roman style. 'As a result,' said Tacitus, 'the nation that used to reject the Latin language began to aspire to rhetoric; further, the wearing of our dress became a distinction, and the toga came into fashion, and little by little the Britons went astray into alluring pastimes: to the promenade, the bath, the well-appointed dinner table.' A Celtic

1. The extreme ends of the Roman world meet up in a windswept spot at Carrawburgh in Northumberland, just south of Hadrian's Wall, where a shrine to the Persian fire god, Mithras, was built.

1

2

culture that repeated Roman campaigns had failed to destroy was now being willingly traded in by the Britons themselves. As Tacitus remarked, 'The simple natives gave the name of "culture" to this factor of their slavery.'

But how serious an enslavement was it? The Romans did keep slaves, but then so had most of the empire's pre-Roman societies, and even if their traditional tribal autonomy was lost, much power within the empire still devolved to the provincial level. Local senates and magistracies might no more represent the common people than their metropolitan model represented Rome's plebs, but Roman government assured consistency and order. The idea that local populations might have a cultural identity that was precious to them would

1. The provision of Roman amenities helped to turn once-rebellious native populations into would-be Romans. Here we see the ruins of the bath complex at Wroxeter, England.

2. Exquisitely wrought in bronze, this key reminds us how much more there was to Roman technology than the great engineering projects for which the empire is remembered.

3. Now no more than an extra tower for St Mary's church, the Roman *pharos*, or lighthouse, at Dover still stands.

3

have been quite alien to the Romans, who never questioned their own supremacy. Nor does it seem to have occurred much to their subjects, who were for the most part only too happy to assimilate themselves into Roman-style societies.

The Roman rainbow

If local populations welcomed the Roman ways, it is only fair to say that the Roman ways were also welcoming to them: the rigidity of institutional structures seems to have made it much easier for 'outsiders' to rise within them. Roman society may have been largely monocultural, with little comprehension of alternative traditions in its midst, but its easy-going multi-ethnicism would put most modern societies to shame.

The emperors Trajan and Hadrian both came from Spain, as did the poet Martial and the philosopher Seneca. By the late 2nd century, public life in Rome was dominated by statesmen from the various North African provinces. The first African emperor, Septimius Severus, was appointed to office in AD 193; later, easterners came to the fore, men from Asia Minor and Syria. What we would call 'racist' attitudes could

1. Legionaries serving on Hadrian's Wall played with this gaming board and dice, discovered during excavations at Corbridge, Northumberland. Similar games whiled away leisure hours across the Roman world.

2. Roman rule involved not only administration, but a total cultural package: these grotesque heads at Leptis Magna, Libya, brought the serpent-headed Medusa myth to a new North African audience.

2

certainly be found (note, for instance, the satirist Juvenal's ill-tempered claim in the 1st century AD that the cultural 'sewage' of Syria and Greece was pouring into Rome, drowning out the city's old traditions and social hierarchies). But the success of so many of these immigrants in rising to the top of Roman society suggests that his was a minority view: in practice, Roman society was open-minded in its attitudes. Later the poet Rutilius Namazianus declared that Rome had 'made for the people of every country a single fatherland…made a city of what had been the world'.

The Roman Empire at its height covered territories that now belong to 33 different sovereign states; the number of distinct peoples and tribes united under its government was far greater. That so many should have come to be ruled by a single imperial state, and also to identify themselves so naturally with it, suggests that Namazianus's claim was really no exaggeration.

THE IMPERIAL STANDARD CITY

Everywhere they went in the course of their campaigning, the Roman legions took with them a standard plan for their overnight camps, a template in which inherited Etruscan tradition dovetailed with Greek precedent and Roman practicality. Stopping at a suitable site, they offered sacrifices to the gods before marking out twin axes crossing to the four points of the compass. Tents were laid out in a strict grid around a central parade ground.

Not only was this design ritually sound and aesthetically pleasing – a canvas version of the ideal Greek city as sketched out by Hippodamus in classical Athens – it was also easily grasped by soldiers working in the field, with no qualifications in architecture or urban planning, but with any amount of military discipline.

This same basic pattern could easily be given more permanent form as a city. Augustus's men had done precisely this when they founded the city of Mérida a century earlier. Now in Spain, Emerita

1

1. These funerary towers at Palmyra, Syria, did more than commemorate the dead: they proclaimed the presence of Roman rule.

2. Built in Ephesus, in what is now Turkey, the Temple of Hadrian could just as easily have been built anywhere in the Roman world.

Augusta, as it was called, became capital of the western Iberian province of Lusitania, consisting largely of what is now Portugal. Although the Roman city has been overbuilt many times since, extensive traces still remain. Instead of a parade ground, the new city was centred on an open forum, around which streets were laid out in regimented squares, sites closest to the centre being reserved for offices and law courts, shrines and temples.

The water supply

Next in importance as public buildings were the city baths. These have not survived in modern Mérida, but baths were vital to the life of any Roman town. Equipped with hot and cold pools and rooms for massage, the baths were ideal places for men to meet friends and business contacts ▷▷

▷ CONCRETE ATTAINMENTS

Of all Rome's contributions to the world, none has made more of a mark – for better or worse – than concrete. It was the Romans who learned how to blend lime or gypsum with an aggregate of stones or rubble, then stir in water to make a rough grey porridge which, when poured into forms, would set hard. Far more flexible than stone, yet almost as strong, concrete could be worked by comparatively unskilled labour; moreover, Roman concrete (the exact recipe for which was lost until modern times) set just as well under water. It could therefore be used in the construction of the crucial docks and harbour basins through which Rome channelled a thriving overseas trade.

The concrete dome of the Pantheon.

Previous page: The backdrop to the stage of the open-air theatre at Mérida, Spain.

1. This public latrine at Ostia was typical of the facilities found throughout the Roman Empire.

2. The distinctive square grid-plan of Roman cities such as Pompeii was reproduced throughout the Roman world.

1

Despite their care over matters of sanitation, the Romans were by no means safe from disease: in the 2nd century AD some cities lost up to a third of their population to epidemics of smallpox.

in a relaxing atmosphere (and, since bathing was often mixed, they might meet prostitutes as well).

A visit to a public latrine was similarly social: men sat on communal benchlike arrangements and chatted away, quite at their ease. A constant flow of water beneath the seats carried away the waste, channelling it into specially constructed sewers.

Water to fill the pools and flush the latrines – and, of course, for everyday domestic use – was brought from distant reservoirs along aqueducts. Mérida boasted no fewer than three of these: the one known today as *Los Milagros* (The Miracles) gives a remarkable sense of slender weightlessness in solid stone, with three arched tiers placed one on top of another. Just as impressive in its way is the city's bridge, whose 60 arches span almost 800 m (2625 ft) across the Guadiana river.

Theatres and monuments

A wealthy city, but by no means untypical, Mérida also had facilities for different types of show: an open-air theatre seating 6000 for conventional dramas, an amphitheatre for gladiatorial contests, and a circus for horse and chariot-racing. These were placed outside the city walls to the south, perhaps because Mérida's military builders found it hard to incorporate their curving structures into the rigidly squared city plan.

A distinctively Roman monument, the triumphal arch of Trajan can still to be seen in Mérida. This would have been only one of many monuments and statues, all aimed at raising the citizens' pride in their city and the empire to which it belonged. Cities identical to Mérida sprang up all over the Roman world. More than just a place for living, the Roman city was a declaration of faith in the Roman way: such cities had no need to respond to local conditions – they drew their inspiration and their civic sustenance from the Roman centre.

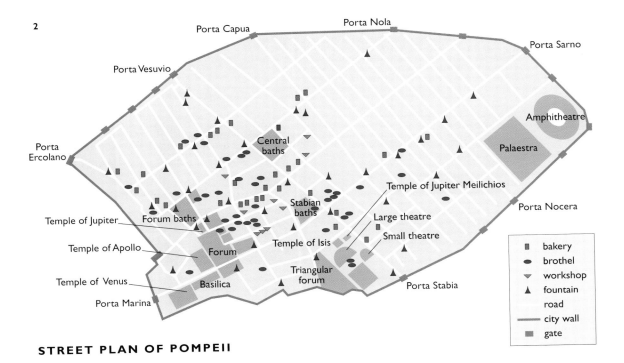

2

Porta Capua
Porta Nola
Porta Sarno
Porta Vesuvio
Porta Ercolano

Central baths

Amphitheatre
Palaestra

Temple of Jupiter Meilichios

Porta Nocera

Stabian baths

Temple of Jupiter
Forum baths
Large theatre

Temple of Apollo
Temple of Isis
Small theatre

Temple of Venus
Triangular forum
Porta Stabia

Porta Marina
Basilica
Forum

Porta Stabia

▪	bakery
●	brothel
▽	workshop
▲	fountain
	road
—	city wall
▪	gate

STREET PLAN OF POMPEII

MAN ABOUT TOWN

If cities were much the same from one end of the empire to the other, so, by and large, was the life led by the typical Roman townsman. His first engagement of the day would be to wait on the wealthy 'patron' with whom he had allied himself, queuing up to be admitted in order of rank, and to receive a daily gift of food, money or advice. In return for this support, he would take his patron's part in any political controversies or lawsuits that might arise – a regular event in a society where everyday life revolved around the assembly and the law courts. An educated and eloquent 'client' could speak up as an advocate for his patron, and even the most tongue-tied could play his part simply by making his support evident in public. While humbly serving his distinguished patron, the typical citizen would almost certainly have clients of his own from further down the social ladder – for this system of patronage permeated Roman society from top to bottom.

Having seen these contacts formally in the morning at their houses and perhaps again in court, the citizen might meet the same people socially in the baths or forum afterwards. One way or another, this daily round took up most of a citizen's time. The whole system seems peculiarly unproductive to modern eyes – but it produced the most powerful social cohesion. The Roman citizen may have had little in the way of democratic power, but he had the strongest possible sense of involvement in the life of his community: *Romanitas* was far more than an ideal – it was an identity.

1

2

1. While a priest makes a sacrifice to Mars, a scribe records names in a census. 'War and Order' was the way of the Roman world.

2. Philosophers argue a point in a relief from a sarcophagus: disputation was the basis of oratory and law, and of all thought.

THE ROMAN HOME

With its colonnaded courts and temples, its spacious streets and central forum, the Roman city bore a distinct similarity to its classical Greek predecessor. Constructed round an open *agora*, a space reserved for walking and talking, Greek cities placed public life and social interaction at the very heart of their culture. To a large extent, the Romans shared the same priorities, as is evident not only from extensive written sources, but also from the care and expense they lavished on every sort of public place – not only *fora*, but baths and theatres, and even latrines. Yet while the Roman citizen liked to play a full part in his community's social and political life, he wanted his home to be his fort: city planning promoted public interaction, but the wealthy house, or *domus*, turned a very cold shoulder to the world.

Like its Greek counterpart, the *domus* confronted life in the street outside with blank exterior walls. Inside, all was airy spaciousness, with rooms arranged around an *atrium* (open court), which might feature mosaics underfoot and frescoes on every wall, as well as a central *impluvium* (pool for rainwater). The family took its meals reclining on couches arrayed around a designated *triclinium* (dining room). This, too, might open out on to an open-air courtyard, though in colder climates it would be fully enclosed.

 THE TOGA

The occasion on which a teenage boy first put on the *toga virilis* was one of the great milestones of his life: the distinctive garment was the uniform of Roman manhood. An understated but eloquent dress-code marked out important social distinctions, the senator's white robe edged with purple a marked contrast to the grubby brown of the ordinary citizen's everyday tunic of undyed wool. Resplendent in his *toga candida* – a dazzling white – the election candidate certainly cut a striking figure. Impressive as it was, though, the toga was difficult to put on, cumbersome to wear and oppressively hot in summer. By the 1st century AD, emperors were having to issue edicts insisting on its use – so vital was it, they felt, to Rome's imperial dignity.

1. The hypocaust at Fishbourne would have brought much-needed comfort to villa life in wind- and rain-swept Britain, providing discreet but effective underfloor heating.

2. This villa in central Italy was typical of similar homesteads throughout the provinces of the Roman Empire. It was at once an economic and administrative centre and a magnate's 'palace'.

The Romans had their own systems of central heating, using a hypocaust. Floors were raised on short pillars, with hot air from a furnace dispersed by convection through the cavity beneath.

A country villa

Divided into large square holdings by 'centuriation', the countryside was as strictly regimented as the town, and the villas of the great rural magnates were strikingly similar in appearance to the great townhouses of the urban rich. The frescoes found at a rural villa at Fishbourne in Sussex would not have been out of place in a wealthy merchant's *domus* in Pompeii or Rome. With so much more space here than in the city, though, the whole place could afford a much looser, more sprawling design.

Although it gives the same impression of opening inward, there is no sense that a country villa had to be fortified against attack: so complete was the *pax Romana* that security could be taken for granted. With its extensive household of family and slaves, a large villa functioned economically as its own micro-city in the countryside, administering the work of the surrounding *latifundium* (plantation) and living on the harvest it produced. In this respect the country villa stood in the same relation to the lands around it, as the city did to its province, or Rome to the empire as a whole.

The splendour of the great Roman houses, whether in the town or in the country, was of course less a matter of immediate comfort than of display. Romans aspired to public influence, and the appearance of substance was all-important.

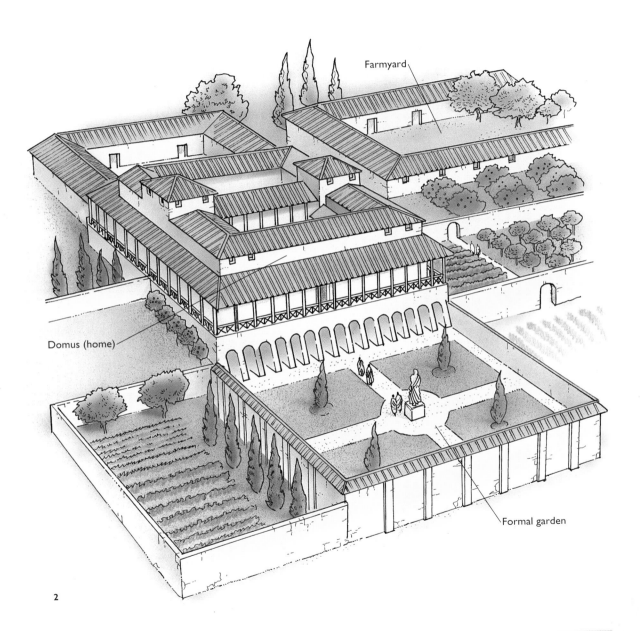

Farmyard

Domus (home)

Formal garden

2

PORTRAIT OF A LADY

The stereotypical Roman family was a small-scale tyranny, the *paterfamilias* (father of the family) having power of life and death over his own children. His wife stayed at home to spin and weave and to serve her husband. The reality could, however, be rather different. With her husband so often away at war, the Roman woman of the upper classes was a queen in her domestic realm – and enjoyed far more autonomy beyond it than her equivalent in classical Greece. Athenian democracy had never extended as far as women: an oppressive etiquette had effectively confined the highest-born wife or daughter to her house. Roman wives, though politically powerless, had considerable personal and financial freedom; they could go out to the baths with female companions, or enjoy a visit to the theatre or the games.

Marriages were arranged by families, with the family's financial fortune and kin-connections very much in view. The notion of romantic love was not unknown, but it was not considered a basis for marriage. Married life was not necessarily joyless, however: love often seems to have grown gradually between husbands and wives. 'You cannot believe how much I miss you,' wrote the historian Pliny the Younger to his wife Calpurnia early in the 2nd century AD. 'I love you so much, and we are not used to separation. So I stay awake most of the night thinking of you. The only time I am free from this misery is when I am in court and wearing myself out with my friends' lawsuits.' Those for whom marriage had not worked out so

1

1. A Roman bride and groom exchange their vows in a 2nd-century AD marriage ceremony, sealing what by historical standards was a remarkably equal partnership.

2. The bigger the empire, the bigger the hair, it seems – as this bust from the Flavian period clearly shows.

3. Re-created daily by teams of specialized maidservants, the glamorous patrician lady was a walking, talking advertisement for her family's power and wealth.

2

3

satisfactorily could always consider going to law themselves: divorce was freely available – for women, increasingly, as well as for men. The actual balance of power between husbands and wives may therefore not have been as unequal as it seems. Conscious of her value as a tradeable commodity, the well-born wife could hold her head high.

Keeping up appearances

The longer the empire went on, the higher the Roman lady seemed to hold her head, thanks to the increasingly extravagant hairstyles that were dictated by fashion. The abundance of surviving statues of female figures has allowed us to follow in some detail the development of Roman hairdressing over several centuries. From the severe styles of the early republic, a gradual elaboration can be traced: the fine lady of the Flavian period (late 1st century AD) was topped by a Colosseum of curls, all meticulously coiffured.

Make-up could be equally elaborate, with foundation made from lanolin, the grease extracted from raw wool, over which a range of earth rouges or pale white lead or chalk was carefully laid. Dark antimony was applied as a form of mascara around the eyes, and filings of haematite and other minerals were used to provide a multicoloured glitter.

The austerity demanded by Roman tradition did to some extent survive in the lady's clothes, and above all in the clear, graceful lines of her *stola* (robe). This would merely have been the foil, however, to set off an array of sumptuous jewellery – diadem, earrings, bracelets, anklets and rings – as

1

2

1. This lady wears jewels typical of 2nd-century AD Roman Egypt. The picture comes from the mask placed over the face of her mummified body.

2. This golden necklace proclaims not only the wealth of its wearer, but the craftsmanship of its Roman maker.

3. A Roman lady bathes her baby with the assistance of a female slave.

well as a coloured *pallium* (outdoor cloak). With her hair looking like a work of art in its own right, and all her gold and jewellery, the rich Roman woman, like her house, was a good advertisement for her family's wealth.

Women of parts

Other lifestyles were, however, available to Roman women. Poorer women or female slaves often found work as seamstresses, washerwomen, cooks, midwives, wet-nurses, healers, actresses and dancers – or served in the empire's extensive sex industry as prostitutes. There were higher-born courtesans as well, two of whom, Astyanassa and Elephantine, were said to be the authors of a popular work of pornography.

Several patrician women wrote more serious works of literature: the memoirs of Nero's mother, Agrippina, were referred to by Tacitus, while in the 1st century AD Pamphile of Epidaurus wrote books on just about every branch of ancient learning. Pliny the Elder lists a number of well-regarded women painters in the 1st century AD. Women are also known to have contributed important work in such fields as philosophy and medicine.

3

A WOMAN SPEAKS OUT

In 42 BC, when the First Triumvirate attempted to introduce a special tax on Roman matrons, one woman, Hortensia, decided to speak out. Invading the sanctified male space of the council chamber, she usurped the ultimate masculine civic role as public orator, addressing the assembled officials with both passion and eloquence. It says something for Roman open-mindedness that, while Hortensia's intervention undoubtedly caused resentment, it aroused admiration too: so much so that she had her way and the tax was rescinded.

METROPOLITAN LIFE

Rome was not, of course, founded and planned by imperial Romans: instead, the whole city sprawled haphazardly outward over the centuries from its Latin origins. Its plan can only be described as chaotic, while the streets themselves were narrow, noisy, filthy and congested. Augustus's boast of having found a city of brick and left it one of marble is true as far as the great state buildings are concerned, but public affluence was accompanied by a great deal of private squalor. Most people lived not in a spacious villa or elegant domus, but crammed into tenements called *insulae* (islands). Often badly built firetraps up to 21 m (70 ft) high,

1

2

1. These stepping-stones in a Pompeii street provided a safe way across a quagmire of rainwater run-off and raw sewage.

2. These old *insulae* in Ostia provide a picture of what life must have been like for ordinary Romans.

3. Construction workers operate a hoist on this relief from a 1st-century AD tomb thought to belong to a family of builders.

with no running water except for those privileged households – often the landlords themselves – who inhabited the ground floor, these buildings were havens for every variety of germ and disease. By the end of the 3rd century AD there were more than 46,000 such *insulae* in Rome, home to many hundreds of thousands of families.

The streets below, foul with garbage and animal and human waste, were unlit at night and almost impassable by day, their pavements – where they existed – blocked by tradesmen's stalls, and roadways thronged by pushing, shoving pedestrians. The rich were borne along in litters, a clean and dry, if rather jerky, ride. Their barging progress through the crowd helped heighten what was already a mood of irritability.

Pedlars and beggars pestered passers-by; whores hustled volubly for business; musicians and entertainers from every corner of the empire added to the pandemonium. Builders yelled to one another from scaffolding overhead, and a householder's shouted warning might be followed by a bucketful of waste. Walking in the streets of ancient Rome cannot have been a pleasant experience.

Safety on the streets

In an attempt to clear the traffic jams, horse or ox-drawn wagons were banned during daylight hours by an edict of Julius Caesar, which was maintained by his imperial successors. This only prolonged the agony for ordinary citizens, though, ensuring as it did an unrelenting cacophony that continued round the clock. 'Who but the rich,' asked the

3

Rome's population of more than a million was not matched by any other European city until London finally overtook it in the 19th century.

satirist Juvenal, 'get any sleep in Rome?…Stand-offs between carts in the narrow, crooked streets; the cursing of drivers brought up short – the doziest of sea-cows couldn't hope to snooze.' Accidents were frequent and, apart from any injury or death caused, often produced traffic tailbacks that could last well into the morning.

Vehicles were not the only danger: crime was rife in the streets, and a pedestrian might just as easily find himself murdered for a laugh by upper-class revellers as mugged for his money by the city's cut-throats. 'This is the highest freedom a poor man can ask,' noted Juvenal bitterly. 'Beaten to a pulp, he must plead to be permitted to return home with just a few of his teeth intact.'

The 'Eternal City'

However, Juvenal also touches on some of Rome's attractions – Trajan's baths, for instance (even if he sees this magnificent complex merely as a stew of sexual licence). The truth is that every emperor since Augustus had embarked on a programme of public works, hoping to improve his own image by making a contribution to the imperial capital. Even as it grew in squalor, the *caput mundi* (head of the world), as Rome was known, grew in grandeur too, every decade adding some new architectural marvel to its catalogue of wonders. The Arch of Titus, the Palace of Domitian, the Circus Maximus, the Pantheon: the list was lengthening all the time.

1. Built at the beginning of the 2nd century AD, Trajan's Forum lent a new dignity to commercial life in Rome, accommodating market stalls in marbled terraces lined with sumptuous statuary.

2. A Roman greengrocer plies his trade, as recorded by a relief on a tomb in Ostia, dating from the 3rd century AD.

THE ROMANS AT WORK AND PLAY

However sublime the monuments among which he worked, the daily life of the average Roman was more prosaic. Although spared the unremitting toil that fell to 90 per cent of the empire's population who had to labour for their living on the land, most urban-dwellers could still expect to work hard – though the rewards could be considerable, too. Even the patrician was kept busy: his round of apparently unpaid 'civic duties' was actually a way of trading influence and amassing bribes.

Further down the social scale came money-lenders, merchants and entrepreneurs in whose factories, workshops or outdoor gangs whole groups of craftsmen and unskilled hands found employment. Metal-workers of every description, jewellers, glassmakers, carpenters, wheelwrights,

2

 THE THEATRE

Overshadowed on the one hand by the great tragedies of ancient Athens and on the other by the bloodier spectacles enacted in Rome's own gladiatorial arenas, Roman drama has not received the attention it deserves. Yet the Romans were great *aficionados* of the theatre. As in Greece, theatrical performances originated in religious festivals and typically involved dance and music. Stately tragedy was performed alongside the most raucously vulgar comedy, male actors taking both men's and women's parts. Masks helped project character and mood to those placed far back in the raked seating; clever mechanisms were designed to facilitate changes of scene. Regarding the Romans' dramatic output, posterity has had mixed feelings: the dazzlingly constructed comedies of Plautus and Terence are revered to this day. The tragedies written later by Seneca strike us as being cheaply sensational in content and overblown in style: yet Shakespeare seems to have prized Roman comedy and tragedy equally.

tanners, spinners, weavers and dyers: the list of industrial occupations is endless. And then there were the butchers, bakers, grocers and other shopkeepers and stallholders, as well as the porters and carters who kept the urban economy moving. Alongside these, a huge construction industry was central to the urban economy, providing opportunities for craft-workers with a vast range of specialized skills.

Of approximately 1.2 million people in the city in the early decades of the 2nd century AD, a third – some 400,000 – were slaves. They were, in effect, the property of others, with no control over their own destinies: it was a complete subjection, though not necessarily a cruel one. While slaves were worked hard on the rural *latifundia*, the urban slave might live no differently (his status apart) from his Roman owner. Serving beside him in his shop, or helping at his workbench, the slave might well be a respected worker in his own right, while household slaves were often regarded with great affection by their patrician families. Some slaves worked in

factories or workshops on equal terms with other hands, the difference being that, when payday came, their wages went directly to their owners. The distinction between the lifestyle of the 'free' Roman and the slave might sometimes be slight when it came to strictly material conditions, but with no legal rights whatsoever, slaves were defenceless in the face of whatever maltreatment an unscrupulous owner might inflict: overwork, sexual exploitation, physical abuse or even murder.

Roman holidays

Hard though they may have worked, however, the Romans knew how to take time off and enjoy themselves. The working day, though it started at dawn, was generally over by early afternoon, and after that there was time to take things easy. This might involve a visit to the baths or gym to tone up the body, or simply socializing with friends, strolling in a public place, or sitting under a shady portico or in a convenient doorway to watch the

1. In a scene from a pavement mosaic, Romans enjoy a banquet to the accompaniment of music.

2. 'Hold me so I can't flee, and return me to my master Viventius': the dog-tag worn by a 4th-century AD slave.

2

world go by. The main meal of the day was in the evening, though only the rich had the facilities to eat at home: most dined at taverns, where they could also drink and gamble well into the evening.

The Roman calendar of festivals and holidays seems strangely chaotic to us. Early Latium observed rituals for honouring ancestors, for giving thanks for the harvest, and for summoning back the spring – which agricultural societies have all tended to share – and from its inception the republic also set apart special days to commemorate important victories. The list of such triumphs grew as Roman power rose, and when the emperors' birthdays and other such dates had also been incorporated, every other day (literally, by the 1st century AD) had become a holiday.

▷ SPIRITUAL LIFE

Rome started out with a recognizably Greek-inspired pantheon of gods and goddesses, in which all-powerful Jupiter (the Greek Zeus), Venus (Aphrodite), Mars (Ares), and so on were honoured in public or private rituals. As its rule extended eastwards, however, the empire's religion became influenced by the Asian religions it encountered – hence a trend towards emperor worship in the 2nd century AD, and the growth of mystery cults. Among the poor, the influence of the early Persian deity Mithras grew fast, as did that of the Egyptian love goddess Isis and the cult of Serapis, compounding Greek and Egyptian mystery traditions. Christianity was only one of many spiritual sects competing for converts in a society that had formerly favoured public observance over private belief: the occasional persecutions of Christians generally stemmed from motives of immediate political expediency.

The games

Among the holiday diversions available to Romans of all classes were increasingly elaborate shows. Up to a quarter of a million people crowded into the Circus Maximus each April to watch the great horse and chariot races – their origins in the rites offered to Ceres, goddess of corn, all but forgotten by imperial times. But the thrills offered by these dangerous contests were surpassed by those of the bloody battles at the Colosseum, where men were pitched against wild (and increasingly exotic) animals in *venationes* (hunts), or in mortal combat as gladiators. The *retiarius* with his net and trident and the *secutor* (pursuer) who dogged him with his shield and sword; the unarmoured but agile *myrmillo*; the

hoplomachus with his giant shield; the *laquearius* with his lasso; the *Thraces* armed, Thracian-style, with short, sickle-like swords – the standard types of gladiator recalled the enemies of early Rome, now tamed and matched against each other in the arena for the entertainment of their conquerors.

Many gladiators were professionals (even a few higher-class citizens are known to have chosen the career voluntarily, perhaps because of the hard-bitten glamour associated with it), but criminals were also sometimes condemned to the gladiator's role as a form of punishment. For most gladiators, the career was a death penalty: few survived long enough to retire and become trainers. In its remote origins of sacred ritual, offering blood to appease the spirits of the dead, the gladiatorial contest

1

1. A charioteer urges on his team as they approach the triple-columned turning-post: chariots often overturned on these 180-degree corners.

2. Gladiators and lions do battle in the arena in this terracotta relief from the 1st century AD.

2

became an affirmation of Roman superiority over warlike barbarian enemies – and ultimately an unholy gratification of the still more bloodthirsty tastes of the civilized Romans.

Theatre of cruelty

It is tempting to moralize about Roman blood-thirstiness, but the Romans did not see things as we do. Even thinkers such as Seneca and Marcus Aurelius, who are known to have disliked gladiatorial contests, seem to have condemned them more for their down-market raucousness than for their inhumanity. The stately dramas written by Seneca show how savage the most educated Roman tastes were: although self-consciously artistic works, they are grotesquely gory by modern standards.

The Romans seem to have had an insatiable hunger for spectacle, lavishing huge sums of money and ingenuity on special effects and showmanship. At one show in the reign of Septimius Severus in the early 3rd century, a vast model whale trundled into the arena and opened its mouth to disgorge 50 bears against a corps of waiting *bestiarii* (hunters) armed with spears. *Naumachiae* were events held in special stadiums with purpose-built aqueducts and drains that allowed arenas to be flooded or drained at will. These events, whose production values were not matched until modern Hollywood went into the re-creation of them, took the form of mock naval battles fought by crews of criminals – with real bloodshed. These spectacles show the Romans at their best and their worst, in both technical accomplishment and casual cruelty.

DECLINE AND FALL

DECLINE AND FALL

As the 2nd century approached its end, Rome stood out as a city of unprecedented size and splendour, the centre of an empire unmatched in scale or order. Moralists eager to connect the empire's ultimate eclipse with 'decadence' have tended to ignore the fact that the flaws they point to had by and large existed every bit as strongly in the vigorously ascendant Rome of republican and early imperial times. The men and women who made Rome great differed little in obvious essentials from those born to serve the empire through the centuries of its decline. Yet, for whatever reasons, the empire did indeed decline – but slowly, and with many great achievements standing out against the general trend until the very end. The Roman story was by no means over. In the east, an evolving empire would endure another thousand years. And in the West, the legacy of Rome would form the intellectual and cultural basis of the modern age.

Previous page: The Forum of Augustus, with the Temple of Mars, still an imposing sight today. After such splendour, could there be any way for Rome but downward?

WHAT USE WAS ROME?

There is no shortage of evidence in Rome itself for those seeking a moralistic explanation for the decline of the Roman Empire. By far the biggest urban settlement the world had ever seen, Rome had many of the social problems of a modern city, exacerbated by huge inequalities of wealth and status. Economically, the city was a net consumer on a massive scale, sucking in the produce of the empire for (many provincials felt) negligible return.

There were those within the city itself who thought no good could come of this unproductive prosperity. Seneca was scathing in his contempt for the conspicuous consumption he saw around him: 'Is it not living unnaturally,' he asked, 'to hanker after roses during the winter, and to force lilies… keeping up the temperature with hot-water heating? Is it not living unnaturally to plant orchards on the top of towers, or to have a forest of trees waving in the wind on the roofs and ridges of one's mansions?' The lavish licentiousness of a Roman orgy may be

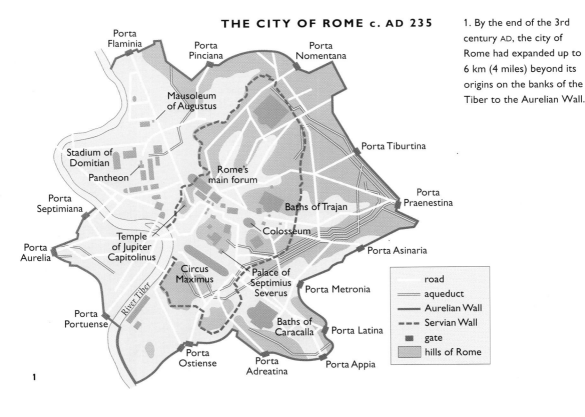

THE CITY OF ROME c. AD 235

- Porta Flaminia
- Porta Pinciana
- Porta Nomentana
- Mausoleum of Augustus
- Stadium of Domitian
- Pantheon
- Rome's main forum
- Porta Tiburtina
- Porta Septimiana
- Porta Praenestina
- Baths of Trajan
- Porta Aurelia
- Colosseum
- Temple of Jupiter Capitolinus
- Porta Asinaria
- Circus Maximus
- Palace of Septimius Severus
- Porta Metronia
- River Tiber
- Porta Portuense
- Baths of Caracalla
- Porta Latina
- Porta Ostiense
- Porta Adreatina
- Porta Appia

Legend:
- road
- aqueduct
- Aurelian Wall
- Servian Wall
- gate
- hills of Rome

1. By the end of the 3rd century AD, the city of Rome had expanded up to 6 km (4 miles) beyond its origins on the banks of the Tiber to the Aurelian Wall.

1

largely fanciful, but the image does seem to have had some basis in fact. A notorious fictional account by Petronius in his *Satyricon* paints an extraordinary picture of one such banquet in the 1st century AD. It is hosted by the self-made millionaire Trimalchio, who is determined to impress all comers.

A fashionable feast

On the menu are hors-d'oeuvres of dormice dipped in honey and sprinkled with poppy seed, as well as pastry peahen's eggs with yolk-dipped figs inside. After this come an array of dishes wittily devised to suggest the signs of the zodiac. As Seneca would have been quick to notice, everything parodies nature at Trimalchio's feast: a hare has chicken's wings attached so as to look like Pegasus, the legendary flying horse, while fish appear to swim in their peppery sauce. As ever more extravagant dishes come thick and fast, the *pièce de résistance* is a giant wild boar, 'hunted' to the table by an escort of baying hounds. The ingenious contrivance doesn't end there, for this male beast is stretched out on a salver as though actually a sow, with piglets of cake laid out as though suckling from her. When its belly is ceremonially opened, a flock of thrushes flies out: nimbly caught by attendant 'huntsmen',

1. (opposite) Roman decadence, as imagined by the French painter Thomas Couture in 1847. While some Romans certainly gave good parties, there is little evidence to suggest that these hastened the city's eventual downfall.

2. That there was some truth in the 'Roman orgies' myth is shown by this wall painting from the 1st century AD – but the Roman artist was quite possibly giving way to

2

they are distributed among the astonished guests. On and on the banquet goes, with fruit in the form of this and cakes shaped like that, while beautiful boys bring 100-year-old wine to keep the party going. Trimalchio's hospitality is outrageously pretentious, but his feast is almost certainly only an exaggeration of what a certain sort of Roman entertainment must really have been like.

To most Romans, though, this bill of fare would have seemed every bit as extraordinary as it does to us: their diet of bread, meat, fish, cheese, pulses and fruit, washed down with a roughish wine, would not have been much different from that of the Mediterranean countries today. Most people ate in local bars. In Pompeii, for example, there are some 200 buildings that are still recognizable as taverns – one even has the price of wine listed on the wall.

Speaking up for the stomach

Did Rome simply consume without giving anything back? This argument recalls Menenius Agrippa's famous fable of the belly. When Rome's populace complained in republican times that the patricians simply exploited their hard labour, the senator told the tale of how the different body parts had risen in mutiny against the stomach.

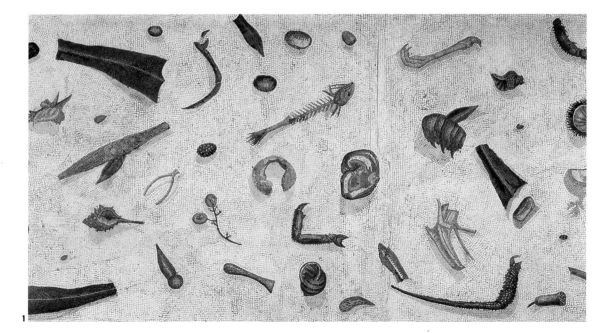

1

2

1. A messy floor, or a work of art? A mosaic floor depicts scraps fallen from a rich man's table.

2. The spirit of revelry run riot, the Roman wine god Bacchus is attended by dancers, cup-bearers and a mischievous Cupid.

PLINY'S BEAUTY TIPS

Asses' milk made the skin glow with youth, noted the historian (and amateur beautician) Pliny the Elder: wealthy women would bathe in it 'up to seven times a day'. Treatments for unsightly spots included the application of cow's placenta (still warm), or a gluey mixture made from calf genitals dissolved in vinegar with sulphur. The supposed self-indulgence and narcissism of rich Roman women in particular is linked by some observers with the empire's later decline. The reality is that wealthy women had been concerned to cultivate a glamorous appearance since the earliest republican times: for better or worse, Rome was always a highly status-conscious society.

But when they refused to give further food to an organ that seemed simply to eat up the products of their hard work, they soon found themselves becoming weakened in their turn. The tale reflects a certain glibness and self-satisfaction on the speaker's part, but it captures the relationship between Rome and its provinces well: how could such an essentially centralized empire function without its centre? Rome's contribution could not be quantified in the way that agricultural and industrial production could, yet without the administrative order it provided, the provinces would clearly have been very much the poorer.

TROUBLE AT THE TOP

For any ambitious Roman, the office of emperor was obviously the greatest prize of all, bringing with it almost unimaginable wealth and influence. Not surprisingly, some individuals for whom imperial power was within reach were prepared to commit any treachery, or any amount of bloodshed, that might help them get to the top. Since the 1st century BC, when the *triumvirs* claimed the authority of the people for themselves, a pattern of

conspiracy, coup and assassination had been established. There were exceptions, of course, with some emperors ruling peacefully for decades at a time, but the potential for violent overthrow – and any number of precedents – was always there.

It did not help that, increasingly, the big political players came from military backgrounds – these were not the orator-statesmen of old, but generals who were accustomed to prevailing through force of arms. When Septimius Severus became emperor in AD 193, he did so at the head of his

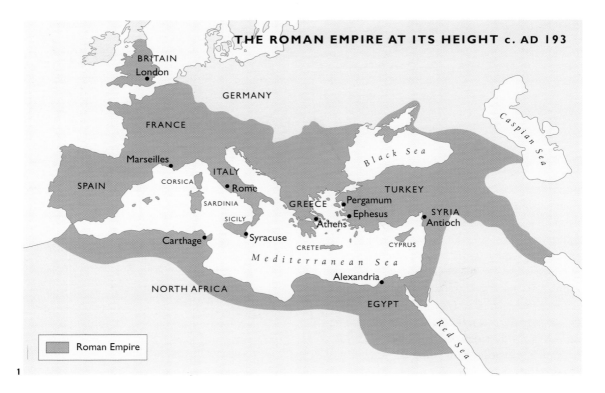

THE ROMAN EMPIRE AT ITS HEIGHT c. AD 193

1

1. The Roman Empire at its height was over 3000 km (2000 miles) across and brought anything from 50 to 100 million people under the authority of a single state.

2. The theatre at Leptis Magna, Libya. Septimius Severus, the first of Rome's African emperors, was born in Leptis Magna, a splendid colonial city with all the amenities of Rome itself.

2

legions, with which he had to fight off the armies of his leading rivals. The endurance of the Severan dynasty until AD 235 presents an historical illusion of easy continuity: in fact, the bickering between Septimius's descendants was unceasing and often murderous. But even this imperial to-ing and fro-ing was insignificant compared to that of the period immediately following the Severans, when power slipped through the hands of a series of 'Barracks Emperors' – no fewer than 21 over a total of 50 years.

Applying technology used in milling, one 4th-century AD Roman inventor devised a paddle-driven warship powered by a pair of oxen.

Diocletian's divisions

The advent of Diocletian in AD 284 brought much-needed stability to the empire: an administrative genius, he divided an empire that was becoming unwieldy into separate, subordinate zones. Power was effectively devolved to three or four sub-emperors, leading to a government that was far more in touch with the growing pressures on the ground. But even these reforms hinted at disintegration in the longer term. As his henchmen fought for the succession in the years following Diocletian's abdication in 305, the empire was indeed broken up for a time, though it was reunited by Constantine in 324. Fighting under the emblem of the Christian cross (which he seems to have embraced at least in part out of political expediency), Constantine saw off his rivals and set himself up as sole ruler of the Roman Empire.

But it did not remain Roman for long: in 330 Constantine transplanted the capital to Byzantium, or Constantinople, several hundred kilometres to the east, on the Bosporus at the heart of the modern Turkish city of Istanbul. Here he was in a better position to deal with the barbarian threat that was menacing the empire from the east – though the western dominions were correspond-ingly neglected. The old imperial heartlands of the west went into a steep decline, with external pressures mounting on every frontier.

1

1. Constantine's vision of the cross became one of the central myths of medieval Christendom. Here it is, as envisaged by a follower of the Italian painter Raphael.

2. This stunning mosaic of Jerusalem was created in the 6th century AD, the artist adapting pagan techniques to Christian ends.

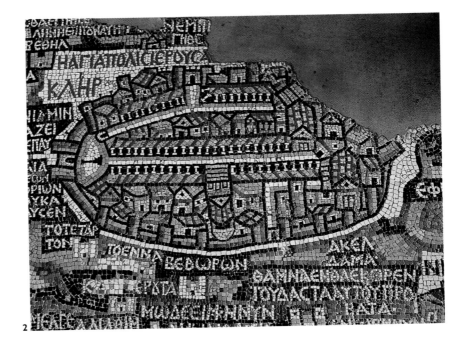
2

 THE DOCTOR'S SURGERY

A people permanently at war inevitably came in for more than its fair share of injuries – and it was not the Roman way to react passively to problems. The same spirit that saw engineers spanning gorges with bridges and traversing marshes with highways was directed inwards by Roman surgeons, who became skilled in the arts of amputation, bone setting and arrowhead removal. Bronze and iron scalpels, saws, probes and forceps were manufactured to impressive standards, but none of this would have been of much consolation to the unfortunate victims, who had to endure treatment with no anaesthetic. Most drugs used by Roman doctors were 'herbal' cures: some may have worked, but others would have been useless.

THE BARBARIANS

The Greek word *bárbaros* reflects what the ancient Greeks perceived as the dominant sound – 'barbar' – of the languages of northern and eastern Europe. Along with the word, the Romans inherited a disdainful attitude towards the so-called 'barbarians'. Far from being an indeterminate, murmuring mass, however, the peoples to whom the term referred comprised a wide variety of distinctive and highly developed societies, even if these were not as technologically advanced as the Romans.

There was huge cultural and linguistic diversity among peoples that ranged from the Picts of Scotland through the Jutes and Saxons of northern Germany to the Goths of central and eastern

1

2

1. This Persepolis relief commemorates the Persians' capture of the Roman emperor Valerian in 260 AD.

2. A Roman cavalry officer rides down a barbarian in this heroic relief: more and more, it seemed, the roles were to be reversed.

Out of the east

In the steppes of Central Asia, nomadic Hun herdsmen followed their flocks across a trackless infinity of grass; they had pursued this way of life for many centuries. The Huns scorned the settled folk whose villages they skirted, though they traded with them when their wealth in wool and hides was in surplus; when it was not, they simply took what they wanted by force. Naturally fitted for the raiding lifestyle, the Huns were expert horsemen and ferocious fighters who travelled light and fast. When population pressures in their Asian homeland forced them further and further westward, Europe was unable to resist them. Their arrival on the Black Sea steppe in around AD 370 sent the Ostrogoths pushing westwards to escape.

The generally peaceful relations that had prevailed along the Roman frontier became destabilized as dislodged Germanic tribesmen sought new lands. The situation was rendered still more dangerous for the empire by the divided loyalties of the legions in that zone. The Roman army had always prided itself on 'Romanizing' foreigners through military discipline, but now the process was starting to operate the other way round. There is evidence that the army itself was becoming 'barbarized' by the high proportion of barbarian troops and officers now within it. Their commitment to the empire and its values could never have been as wholehearted and unconditional as that of the original Roman troops. As its defences were being strained externally, the empire was also crumbling from within.

Europe. The Goths were subdivided into distinct Visigothic (western) and Ostrogothic (eastern) nations, the former living along the Danube, and the latter extending eastwards into the Ukraine. Many of these populations had been in contact with Roman ways for generations, trading with the empire for luxuries, and taking what suited them from 'civilization' while holding fiercely to their distinct heritages. The Romans' fear and distrust may have been exaggerated, but at least one enemy who lived up to the scare stories of barbarian menace appeared from the east.

FINAL STRUGGLE

Mounting military tensions reached their breaking point at the Battle of Adrianople in AD 378. The onslaught of the Huns across southern Ukraine had pushed the Ostrogoths ever farther westwards, and their impact had forced the Visigoths into direct conflict with Rome from 376 onwards. Roman hopes of a diplomatic solution, by admitting the Visigoths into the Roman lands on condition that they disarmed, were dashed when corrupt officials attempted to profiteer by demanding heavy bribes, and Roman attempts to close the frontier failed. Bands of Visigoths, joined by Roman deserters and groups of Huns and Alans, defeated the local Roman troops and spread throughout Thrace (the southern Balkans). In AD 378, misled by faulty reports of Goth numbers, the emperor Valens attempted a decisive blow against their encampment outside the city of Adrianople (modern Edirne, in European Turkey). The Gothic cavalry, absent when the Roman assault began,

1. A hirsute barbarian attacks a clean-cut legionary outside an appropriately primitive-looking hut. It had once apparently been Rome's destiny to bring 'civilization' to such people.

2. A scene from the obelisk of Theodosius, AD 390, shows the emperor receiving the homage of barbarian tribes. The balance of power was soon to shift to Rome's disadvantage.

returned to surround and rout the imperial army: Valens was killed, with some 40,000 of his best troops, in the greatest Roman defeat since Cannae. The Goths thereafter settled permanently within the empire's boundaries, and Rome was no longer able to defend itself without their aid.

A deathbed conversion

Theodosius the Great, Valens' successor, managed briefly to restore stability to the empire, partly by allowing the Goths to remain in Thrace under their own laws in return for military service. One instrument that he used to re-create a semblance of Roman dignity was Christianity, which he made the exclusive creed of the empire in a decree of AD 380. The Church had developed considerably since its first foundation in the empire, but its security as a Roman institution – in the Western empire at any rate – was shortlived.

After a breakdown in relations with their former employer, the Visigoths under Alaric sacked Rome itself in 410, which was both a strategic and symbolic blow. A Hun invasion under Attila was defeated by a Roman and Visigothic army at Châlons in 451, but the Huns returned the following year to invade Italy. One imperial humiliation followed another, until the end came in 461. The last, powerless 'emperor', Romulus Augustulus, found himself formally dethroned by Flavius Odoacer, chief of the Heruls – who simply informed the Eastern emperor Xeno that his representative in the west was no longer needed. Such was the ignominious conclusion to which the grandeur of Rome had come.

2

Britain was one of the first Roman provinces to be lost, in AD 406, when the legions stationed there had to be withdrawn to defend the heart of the continental empire.

THE LEGACY

The Romans were by no means finished, in the sense that the empire in the east survived for another 1000 years. Known as the Byzantine Empire, this state, though fundamentally Greek rather than Roman, kept many of the old Roman values and ways alive. As the troubles further east subsided, and traders in silks and spices replaced the invading bands, the commercial and cultural focus of the world shifted significantly: Byzantine civilization took on a distinctively cosmopolitan – even oriental – feel. In many ways, the Byzantine Empire's very openness to other traditions has served it badly in the historical record. In western historiography, at least, it still remains something of a forgotten empire.

That could never be said of Rome or the Western Empire. Awed by the bridges, aqueducts and temples he saw, one Anglo-Saxon poet concluded that they must be 'the work of giants'. In some ways, this is how we regard the Romans even now: two millennia later, their achievements still seem miraculous. Although the Roman culture was eclipsed for a long time, in the Renaissance it became the intellectual mainstay of modernity. In art, engineering, law and government, and in so much else, the Romans built the foundations of the world.

1. The beautiful work of the Byzantine painter in this portrait of an important official and his wife brings home to us the humanity of those who lived what we too easily dismiss as 'ancient history'.

2. (opposite) The 6th-century emperor Justinian, halo blazing, humbly bears the paten, or plate of consecrated bread, from the Mass: the idea of the Roman Empire would increasingly be subsumed into that of 'Christendom'.

FURTHER INFORMATION

BOOKS

Auguet, Roland, *Cruelty and Civilization: The Roman Games* (London: Routledge, 1994). An intriguing exploration of the more sinister side of Roman civilization, which is revealed by its often gory shows and games.

Boardman, John, *The Oxford History of Classical Art* (Oxford: OUP, 1993). A clear, generously illustrated account of Rome's marvellous achievements in art and their context in the artistic history of the classical world.

Carcopino, Jérome, tr. E.O. Lorimer, *Daily Life in Ancient Rome: The People and the City at the Height of the Empire* (London: Penguin, 1991). First published in 1941, this book is still to be surpassed as a vivid portrait of everyday life in antiquity's greatest city.

Claridge, Amanda, *Rome, An Oxford Archaeological Guide* (Oxford: OUP, 1998). A clear and illuminating guide to the incredible archaeological heritage of Rome itself.

Ferrill, Arther, *The Fall of the Roman Empire: The Military Explanation* (London: Thames & Hudson, 1983). A commonsense consideration of a much-overtheorized period of Roman history.

Finley, M.I., *The Ancient Economy* (Harmondsworth: Penguin, 1992). First published in 1973,

this book still stands unrivalled as a readable general introduction.

Hackett, General Sir John (ed.), *Warfare in the Ancient World* (London: Sidgwick & Jackson, 1989). A highly informative guide to the hardware, tactics and military culture of all the great ancient armies.

Liberati, Anna Maria, and Bourbon, Fabio, *Splendours of the Roman World* (London: Thames & Hudson, 1996). An excellent and beautifully illustrated general account of all the main aspects of Roman history, society and culture.

Lefkowitz, Mary R. and Fant, Maureen B., *Women's Life in Greece and Rome: A Sourcebook in Translation* (London: Duckworth, 1982). Full of unexpected insights into how ancient women led their lives.

Salway, Peter, *Roman Britain: A Very Short Introduction* (Oxford: OUP, 2000). A clear and readable (and admirably brief!) overview of the fascinating story of the Romans in Britain.

Scarre, Christopher, and Fagan, Brian, M., *Ancient Civilizations* (Harlow: Longman, 1997). The Romans themselves get relatively short shrift here, but this book remains invaluable for readers wishing to set their story in the context of other early civilizations worldwide.

INDEX

Italic type denotes illustrations